The Illustrated Rules of
BASEBALL

By Dennis Healy

Illustrated by Patrick T. McRae

Ideals Children's Books • Nashville, Tennessee

For my son, Dennis F. Healy, who has dedicated his life to young people in education and athletics.
—D.H.

For my children, Ryan, Emily, and Alex.
—P.T.M.

Special thanks to the Southwest Little League Padres of 1994: Mike Belich, Paul Bowe, Rick Fox, Mike Gardner, Tylor Huismann, Ben Johnson, Ian Johnson, Ryan McRae, Billy Newburry, Kent Pierson, Adam Schlusser, Bryan Schultz, Jared Stengel, Tristan Thomas, and umpire Eric Barczak.

Published by Ideals Children's Books
An imprint of Hambleton-Hill Publishing, Inc.
Nashville, Tennessee 37218

Printed and bound in Mexico

Library of Congress Cataloging-in-Publication Data
Healy, Dennis.
    The illustrated rules of baseball / by Dennis Healy ; illustrated by Patrick T. McRae.
        p.   cm.
    ISBN 1-57102-017-9
    1. Baseball—Rules—Juvenile literature. 2. Baseball—Juvenile literature. 3. Baseball—Terminology—Juvenile literature. [1. Baseball—Rules.] I. McRae, Patrick, ill. II. Title.
    GV877.H49   1995
    796.357'02'022—dc20   94-32773
                                                            CIP
                                                            AC

Reviewed and endorsed by USA Baseball.

USA Baseball is the National Governing Body (NGB) for amateur baseball, representing the sport at all levels of competition from local youth games to the Olympic Games. USA Baseball's member groups include Little League Baseball, Inc., American Legion Baseball, American Baseball Coaches Association (ABCA), and National Collegiate Athletic Association (NCAA), as well as almost every other amateur baseball organization in the United States.

For more information about the game and opportunities for young players, contact USA Baseball at 2160 Greenwood Avenue, Trenton, New Jersey 08609.

Table of Contents

The Game of Baseball 5

The Rules of the Game..6

The Players 22

Umpire's Signals 28

Sportsmanship in the Game of Baseball 30

Summary of the Rules of Baseball.........................31

Vocabulary of the Game 32

Note to Parents:

The Illustrated Rules of Baseball introduces young players to the basic rules of the game. The rules are presented in a simplified form and are accompanied by detailed illustrations for added clarity. Included is the information that is thought to be of most interest to young players. Designed specifically for the younger player, the fact-filled text and informative illustrations provide a basis for the discussion of the game by players, coaches, and parents.

The rules in this book were written by an experienced amateur baseball coach and umpire who also played Major League Baseball. The author drew not only from his own experience in baseball, but also from baseball tradition and widely accepted rules that are used in various forms by virtually all youth baseball organizations.

The Game of Baseball

Many people think of the game of baseball as America's national pastime. It's hard to imagine summer without it.

Baseball is played by millions of people of all ages. It is played not just in the United States but in some one hundred countries around the world. Baseball is now an Olympic sport and has become popular in Asia and Latin America. It is also becoming more and more popular in Oceania, Europe, and Africa.

The object of the game is simple. One team's pitcher throws the ball to the other team's batter. The batter tries to hit the ball by swinging a bat at it. When the ball is hit, the batter runs to first base, then second base, third base, and finally to home plate. When a runner crosses home plate, a run is scored. But while the runner is trying to safely reach each base, the pitcher's team is trying to get him or her out. After three outs, the teams switch sides. The team with the most runs at the end of the last inning wins the game.

In American Major League Baseball, the best team in the American League meets the best team in the National League at the end of the season in October to play the World Series. The first team to win four games out of seven is declared the best team in baseball . . . until the next year's World Series.

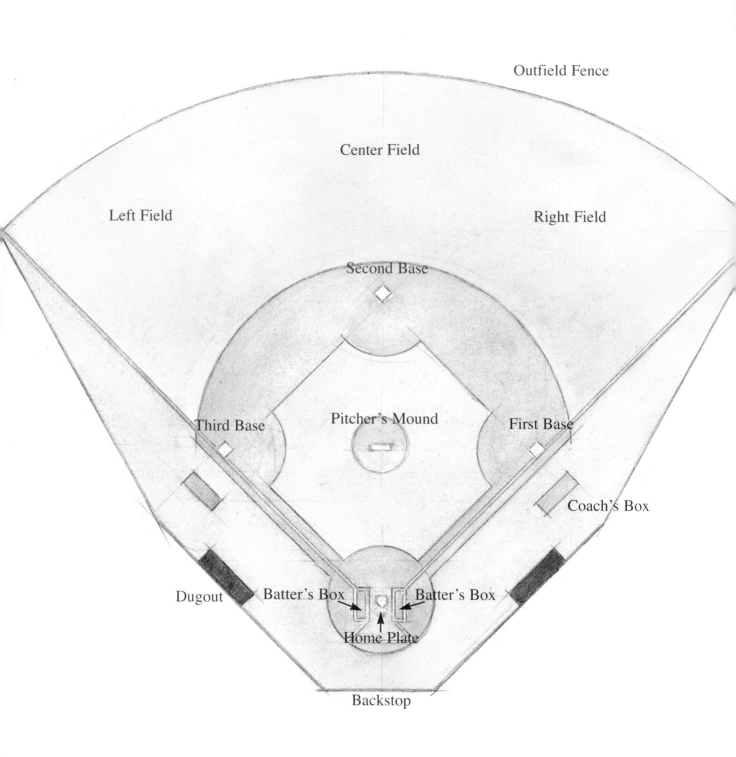

Outfield Fence

Center Field

Left Field

Right Field

Second Base

Third Base

Pitcher's Mound

First Base

Coach's Box

Dugout

Batter's Box

Batter's Box

Home Plate

Backstop

The Rules of the Game

Rule 1: The Field of Play

The baseball field is called a **diamond** because of its shape. The diamond is the area of the field formed by the four bases. Home plate is at the bottom corner, first base is at the right corner, second base is at the top corner, and third base is at the left corner.

The distance from each base to the next depends on the size of the diamond. A youth league diamond is much smaller than a professional diamond. On a diamond for youth leagues of players 12 years or younger, the bases are typically 60 feet apart. The **pitcher's mound** is in the center of the diamond, 46 feet from home plate. On a professional field, the bases are 90 feet apart, and the pitcher's mound is 60 feet 6 inches from home plate.

Each field also has an **outfield fence**. The height of the fence and its distance from home plate also vary according to the size of the field. On a typical youth league field, the outfield fence is 4 feet tall and 200 feet from home plate.

Rule 2: The Ball

The official ball weighs between 5 and $5\frac{1}{4}$ ounces and is between 9 and $9\frac{1}{4}$ inches in **circumference** (the distance around the outside of the ball). Yarn is wound tightly around a small cork or rubber center. This center is then covered with white horsehide or cowhide and stitched together.

For youth leagues, the ball is the same size, but it may be made of different materials and have a synthetic cover.

Rule 3: The Bat

The bat is a smooth, rounded stick made of one piece of solid wood or metal. It can be up to 42 inches long, but not more than $2\frac{3}{4}$ inches wide at the widest point. Youth baseball leagues, high school players, and college-age leagues almost always use bats made of aluminum or other metal alloys, but in professional baseball only wooden bats are allowed.

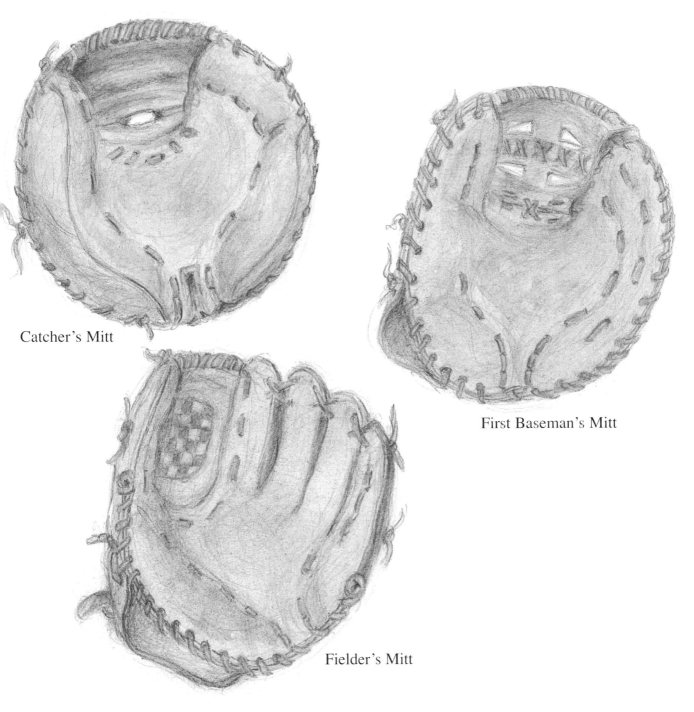

Catcher's Mitt

First Baseman's Mitt

Fielder's Mitt

Rule 4: The Glove

There are three basic types of baseball gloves, also called **mitts**: a catcher's mitt, a first baseman's mitt, and a fielder's mitt. Major league players use gloves made of leather, while younger players may use gloves made of leather or other materials.

Jersey

Pants

Helmet

Cap

Batting Gloves

Socks

Stirrups

Shoes

Rule 5: Other Equipment

Each team has its own uniform, and it must be worn by every player on the team. Each player also wears a number on the back of the uniform so that officials and fans can easily identify the player. Most players wear shoes with **cleats**, or rounded spikes, on the bottom so that they don't slip while running. In youth leagues, these spikes must be nonmetal.

The batter wears a helmet which has double earflaps and may also have a face shield. The helmet protects his or her head from being hit by a pitch. Players in the on-deck batting area and the base runners also wear helmets. The other players in the field wear caps.

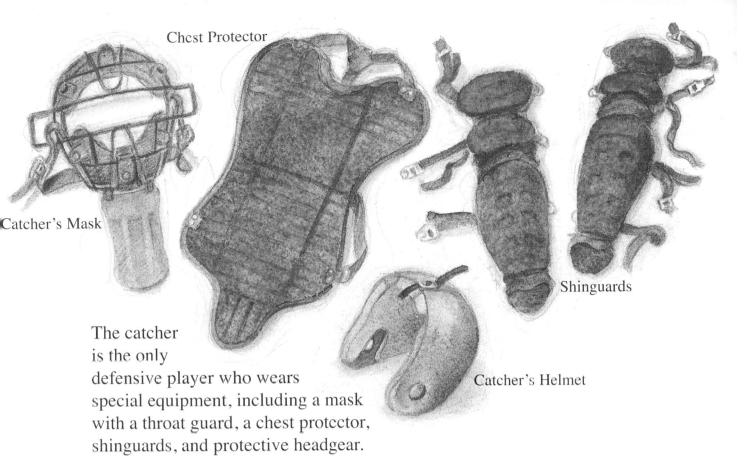

Chest Protector

Catcher's Mask

Shinguards

Catcher's Helmet

The catcher is the only defensive player who wears special equipment, including a mask with a throat guard, a chest protector, shinguards, and protective headgear.

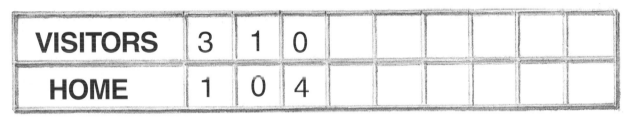

VISITORS	3	1	0						
HOME	1	0	4						

Rule 6: Length of the Game (or Innings)

The game of baseball is usually divided into nine **innings**. Younger players often play fewer innings, with games ranging from five to seven innings. During an inning, each team has a turn playing offense and then defense. After each team has batted and has gotten three outs, an inning is over. After all innings are played, the team which has the most runs, or points (see Rule 17), wins the game. If the score is tied, extra innings are played. As soon as one team is ahead at the end of an extra inning, the game is over.

Left Fielder

Rule 7: The Players

The pitching team, or **defensive** team, has nine players on the field: the pitcher, catcher, first baseman, second baseman, shortstop, third baseman, left fielder, center fielder, and right fielder. The batting team, or **offensive** team, sends one batter at a time to face the pitcher.

Rule 8: The Officials

There are one or more **umpires** for each game. They enforce the rules and their decisions are final. One umpire, the main official, stands behind the catcher. This umpire determines whether a pitch is a "strike" or a "ball" (see Rules 11 and 14). The other umpires decide if runners are "out" or "safe" (see Rules 13 and 18).

Center Fielder

Right Fielder

Umpire

Second Baseman

Shortstop

First Baseman

Pitcher

Third Baseman

Batter

Catcher

Umpire

Rule 9: Batter's Box

The batter takes his or her position in the **batter's box**, which is the area in which the batter stands while at bat. The batter is called the **batter-runner** from the time the ball is hit until the time he or she is either put out or arrives safely on first base. After safely reaching first base, the player then becomes a **runner**.

Right-Handed Batter's Box

Left-Handed Batter's Box

Rule 10: Strike Zone

The pitcher must throw the ball into the **strike zone**. The strike zone is determined by the batter's stance as the batter is preparing to swing at a pitched ball. The upper limit of the zone is a horizontal line that crosses halfway between the top of the batter's shoulders and the top of the uniform pants. The lower limit is a line at the top of the knees.

Strike Zone

Rule 11: Strikes

If the batter swings at a ball and misses, it is called a **strike**. It is also a strike if the batter does not swing at a pitch that was thrown in the strike zone. A foul ball can also be a strike (see Rule 15).

Rule 12: Pitching Positions

There are two positions a pitcher may take before pitching a ball. One is the **windup position**. The other is the **set position**. The windup position is the most common. If a runner is on base, however, the set position is most often used because the time it takes to wind up might allow the runner to steal a base.

Windup Position

Set Position

Rule 13: Outs

A batting team is allowed three **outs** during an inning. When a player is out, he or she must **retire** from the inning. This means that the player sits on the bench and does not play until it is his or her turn in the batting order again. There are many different ways to get a player out. The following are the three most common types of outs.

1. A batter who gets three strikes (see Rule 11) without getting a hit is out. This is called a **strikeout**.
2. If a batter hits the ball and attempts to run to first base, but the ball is thrown to the base before he or she gets there, the batter is out.
3. If the batter hits a ball and the ball is caught before it touches the ground, the batter is out.

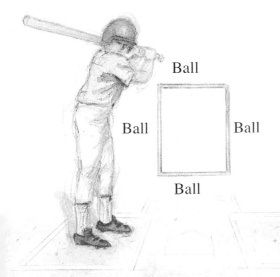

Ball

Ball   Ball

Ball

Rule 14: Base on Balls

A **ball** is a pitch which does not enter the strike zone and is not struck at by the batter. If the pitcher throws four balls, the batter is given a **base on balls**, or a **walk**, and advances to first base.

Rule 15: Fair Territory and Foul Territory

Fair Territory

Foul Territory   Foul Territory

Third Baseline

First Baseline

Fair territory is that part of the playing field within and including the first baseline and the third baseline all the way to the outfield foul poles. **Foul territory** is that part of the playing field outside the first and third baselines. A ball hit into foul territory is a **foul ball**. The first two foul balls count as strikes for a batter. Any foul balls that follow do not count as strikes.

Rule 16: Hits

If the batter hits the ball into fair territory, it is a **hit**. The batter must then run to first base before the ball is thrown to the first baseman in order to be safe (see Rule 18). A runner who is safe on base can advance to the next base if the next batter gets a hit or a walk, or if a member of the other team makes an error (see Rule 19). If the runner is fast, he or she can sometimes advance two or more bases. If a batter hits a home run, any other runners already on base also run home and score.

Rule 17: Runs

A **run** is scored when a player advances around the diamond, touching first, second, third, and home bases in that order. Each run counts as one point.

If the ball is hit far enough, the batter may be able to run safely all the way to second base, third base, or even to home plate. A hit that allows the batter to run to first base is called a **single**, while a hit that lets the batter run to second base is a **double**. If the batter can get to third base without being put out, it is a **triple**. If the batter can run the entire way around the diamond, it is called a **home run**. A ball that is hit over the outfield fence is also a home run. A **grand slam home run** is a home run hit when there are already three players on base. This will score four runs, or four points, the largest number of runs possible from one hit.

Rule 18: Safe on Base

A runner is **safe** on base if he or she touches the base before the fielder who has the ball touches either the runner or the base.

Rule 19: Errors

An error is a mistake by the defensive team that allows the batter-runner to reach first base safely or to advance to the next base. It is an error when a player drops a ball batted in the air or fumbles a batted or thrown ball. It is also an error if the pitcher throws a wild pitch; that is, a pitch which is so high, so low, or so wide of the plate that the catcher cannot reach it.

Fumble

Runner

Rule 20: Stolen Base

A runner may **steal** a base by advancing to the next base without the help of a walk, an error, or a teammate's hit. The most common time for a runner to steal a base is when a ball is pitched to a batter. If the runner is **tagged**, or touched, by a member of the opposing team with the ball, the runner is then out. Most youth leagues do not permit stealing bases, but many leagues for older players do.

The Players

It is important that a player on a youth baseball team play many positions in order to discover what he or she does best. For example, those who play first base or second base do not have to have strong throwing arms. The taller player who has a weak arm, but catches well, may be good at playing first base. A player who has a weak arm, but catches ground balls well, may be better suited for playing second base.

In youth baseball, an outstanding pitcher may also play shortstop, catcher, or outfielder. These are all positions that require strong throwing arms.

As a young baseball player advances in age, he or she will settle into one or two positions. By college age, a player will know whether he or she is a pitcher or an "everyday player." An everyday player may play every day, while a pitcher is limited to a specific number of innings or pitches in a certain amount of time. The pitcher's playing time is limited in order to avoid the injuries that may be caused by pitching too frequently.

The Catcher

The **catcher** must be a good thrower in order to put out runners who are trying to "steal" bases. The catcher must also be able to work well with the pitcher and to help the pitcher decide what kind of pitches to throw.

The Pitcher

The **pitcher** must be strong and have good aim in order to throw the ball into the strike zone. In some leagues, the pitcher is not required to hit, so hitting skills are less important for the pitcher who plays in those leagues.

The Infielders

Many who play first base are tall and long-limbed. This allows them to stretch and catch a ball thrown by another **infielder** just before a batter reaches first base.

Those who play second base, third base, and shortstop—also called infielders— must have quick reflexes in order to catch balls hit sharply toward them. They must be strong enough to throw the ball to first base in order to get runners out.

The Outfielders

The three **outfielders** must be fast enough to cover the large outfield. Speed is essential in order to run down a fly ball hit between the infielders. The outfielders must also be very strong and accurate throwers in order to throw the ball back to the infield as quickly as possible.

Umpire's Signals

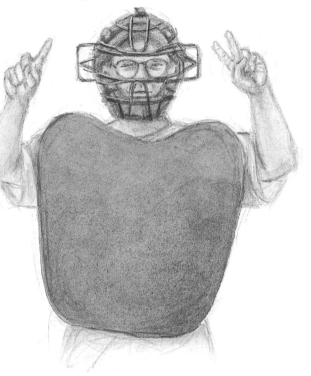

After each pitch, the home plate umpire holds the correct number of fingers up to show the current number of balls and strikes. The number of strikes is always shown on the right hand, while the number of balls is shown on the left.

2 Balls, 1 Strike

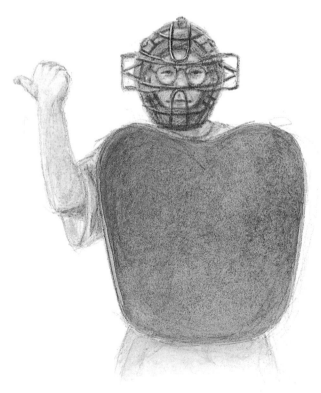

Out

The signal shown at left is the traditional signal given as the umpire calls to the batter or runner, "You're out!" In some leagues, the home plate umpire may use a stronger gesture (called "punching out the batter") to signal that a batter is out: the right fist is punched forward and the left fist is pulled back as the umpire calls, "Strike three, you're out!"

To signal that a runner is safe, the umpire begins with arms close to the chest, then spreads them out. At the same time, the umpire calls out, "Safe!"

Safe

Sportsmanship in the Game of Baseball

A good baseball player shows respect to the other players, coaches, and officials—and to the members of the opposing team. For while it is valuable to learn how to compete, it is even more important to learn how to compete fairly: to try one's best and to follow the rules. This is known as good sportsmanship.

Remember that the umpire's decisions are final. It is poor sportsmanship to argue with the umpire about calls, such as whether a runner is safe or out, or whether a ball has gone into fair or foul territory. It is poor sportsmanship to shout from the dugout at a player who is at bat. A player who wants to be a good sport will not show anger by throwing down the bat or other equipment. He or she will even learn how to lose with grace.

The most important thing to remember when playing baseball is to have fun. It is not necessary to "win at any cost." Parents and coaches should understand this too. They should not shout at the players or argue with the umpires. By their behavior, they can help young players learn to love the game of baseball.

Summary of the Rules of Baseball

Rule 1: The Field of Play
The baseball field is in the shape of a diamond and has four bases—first, second, third, and home plate. The pitcher's mound is in the center of the diamond. Each field also has an outfield fence.

Rule 2: The Ball
The official ball weighs between 5 and $5\frac{1}{4}$ ounces and is between 9 and $9\frac{1}{4}$ inches in circumference.

Rule 3: The Bat
The bat is a smooth, rounded stick made of wood, aluminum, or other metal alloy. It can be up to 42 inches long, but not more than $2\frac{3}{4}$ inches wide at the widest point.

Rule 4: The Glove
There are three basic types of baseball gloves, also called mitts: a catcher's mitt, a first baseman's mitt, and a fielder's mitt.

Rule 5: Other Equipment
A player's equipment includes a uniform with a number on the back, shoes with cleats, and a cap. The batter and the base runners wear helmets. The catcher wears a mask, a chest protector, and shinguards.

Rule 6: Length of the Game (or Innings)
The game of baseball is usually divided into nine innings. After each team has batted and has gotten three outs, an inning is over.

Rule 7: The Players
The pitching team, or defensive team, has nine players on the field. The batting team, or offensive team, sends one batter at a time to face the pitcher.

Rule 8: The Officials
There are one or more umpires for each game. They enforce the rules and their decisions are final.

Rule 9: Batter's Box
The batter's box is the area in which the batter stands during his or her time at bat.

Rule 10: Strike Zone
The pitcher must throw the ball into the strike zone. The strike zone is determined by the batter's stance.

Rule 11: Strikes
If the batter swings at a ball and misses, it is called a strike. It is also a strike if the batter does not swing at a pitch that was thrown into the strike zone. A foul ball can be a strike.

Rule 12: Pitching Positions
There are two positions a pitcher may take before pitching a ball. One is the windup position. The other is the set position.

Rule 13: Outs
A batting team is allowed three outs during an inning. There are many different ways to get an out.

Rule 14: Base on Balls
A ball is a pitch which does not enter the strike zone and is not struck at by the batter. If the pitcher throws four balls, the batter is given a base on balls, or a walk, and advances to first base.

Rule 15: Fair Territory and Foul Territory
Fair territory is that part of the playing field within and including the first baseline and the third baseline all the way to the outfield poles. Foul territory is that part of the playing field outside the first and third baselines.

Rule 16: Hits
If the batter hits the ball into fair territory, it is a hit.

Rule 17: Runs
A run is scored when a player advances around the diamond, touching first, second, third, and home bases in that order.

Rule 18: Safe on Base
A runner is safe on base if he or she touches the base before the fielder who has the ball touches either the runner or the base.

Rule 19: Errors
An error is a mistake by the defensive team that allows the batter-runner to reach first base safely or to advance to the next base.

Rule 20: Stolen Base
A runner may steal a base by advancing to the next base without the help of a hit by a teammate, a walk, or an error.

Vocabulary of the Game

base: one of four points on the field which the runner must touch in order for a run to be scored

base hit: a hit which allows the batter to reach first base safely

bases loaded: runners on first, second, and third bases

batter: the offensive player who stands in the batter's box and tries to hit the pitched ball by swinging a bat at it

battery: the combination of the pitcher and the catcher

doubleheader: two games played back to back

double play: two runners are put out on one play

fielder: any defensive player

fly ball: a batted ball that goes high in the air, usually to the outfield

ground ball: a batted ball that rolls or bounces along the ground

line drive: a batted ball that goes sharp and direct from the bat to a fielder without touching the ground

lineup: or batting order; the order in which the team members bat

pitch: the delivery of the ball from the pitcher to the batter

pitcher's mound: the area from which the pitcher throws the ball to the batter

play: any action that occurs between two pitches

pop-up: a batted ball that goes high in the air in or near the infield

put out: or throw out; the retiring of a batter or a runner

tag: to touch the runner with the ball

triple play: three runners are put out on one play

wild pitch: a pitch so high, so low, or so wide of home plate that the catcher cannot reach it